Rea

Typescripts, proofs and indexes

Judith Butcher

Cambridge University Press

Cambridge

London   New York   New Rochelle
Melbourne   Sydney

Published by the Press Syndicate of the University of Cambridge
The Pitt Building, Trumpington Street, Cambridge CB2 1RP
32 East 57th Street, New York, NY 10022, USA
296 Beaconsfield Parade, Middle Park, Melbourne 3206,
Australia

First published 1980

Printed in Great Britain at the University Press, Cambridge

Library of Congress cataloguing in publication data
Butcher, Judith.
Typescripts, proofs and indexes.
(Cambridge authors' and publishers' guides)
1. Manuscript preparation (Authorship).   I. Title.
II. Series.
PN160.B8   808'.02   79-52666
ISBN 0 521 29739 7

Contents

Every author wants his work to be produced and published without undue delay and to be clear and intelligible to the reader. These aims are more likely to be achieved if the typescript is accurate, consistent and well presented. This booklet shows how you, the author, can help your publisher, the typesetter and the eventual reader by thinking about presentation before the final draft is typed, by correcting proofs efficiently and economically, and by making a really useful index.

The typescript

The typescript must be complete, accurate, clear and consistent. It should represent your final thoughts, not a rough draft to be amended later. Once the book has been typeset, it is expensive to change even a comma.

Three copies should be made. If your publisher has a second copy, he can use it to obtain typesetters' estimates while the master copy is being edited; the second copy can also be used by the marketing department. You should always keep a fully corrected copy yourself, both as an insurance against loss and to help you to answer queries about the text.

The manuscript should be typed in a consistent type size on a good-quality A4 or quarto bond paper, with a ribbon that gives a clear black impression. Only one side of the sheet should be used, and all the sheets must be the same size. The copy to be sent to the typesetter must be the 'top' (ribbon) copy; a carbon copy will become blurred when it is handled, and some photocopies are so faint as to be almost illegible.

There should be margins of at least $1\frac{1}{2}$ inches (40 mm) at the left, and of 1 inch (25 mm) at the top, the right and the foot; the publisher and typesetter need this space for their own marking-up.

Everything should be double-spaced, including quotations, notes and references, to allow room for corrections or any editorial marking.

Notes should be numbered serially through each chapter. Unless it has been agreed that the notes are to be printed at the foot of the relevant page of text (see p. 14) they should be typed on separate sheets placed after the text and any appendixes. The notes for each chapter should start on a fresh sheet with 'Notes to Chapter *x*' at the top. Footnotes may be treated in the same way or may be typed, *double-spaced*, in the main text at the foot of the page containing the footnote indicator.

Chapters should be numbered in arabic, and each one should start on a fresh sheet.

The first line of each paragraph should be indented unless it follows either a heading occupying a separate line or a gap between paragraphs to show a change of subject. Where such a gap is needed, write 'space' in the margin; this is particularly important if one of these breaks falls at the foot of a page.

Words should not be broken at the ends of lines; if they are, the typesetter may be uncertain whether the word should be set with a hyphen.

The typist should distinguish between II, 11 and the abbreviation ll. (lines). If the typewriter has no 1 any ambiguous cases must be identified; similarly with capital O and zero. Any handwritten material such as mathematics and non-roman characters, must be clear and unambiguous, with subscripts and superscripts clearly positioned (see also p. 20). A list of any special symbols or letters should be provided and photocopies of such characters as they appear in printed works are valuable to show the printer exactly what is needed.

Corrections and additions should be typed. Occasional words may be legibly handwritten in in between the lines (*not* in the margin), but do not use a thick felt-tip pen. Where there are larger additions retype the pages affected. Do not use transparent tape, pins or staples to attach new material: the new material may hide what is below it; it is impossible to write over most transparent tapes; pins can become detached; and staples may catch in the typesetter's copy-holder. If the typescript is not completely legible, or additions are written up the margin or on the back of the sheet, the typesetter will have to take the sheet out of the holder in order to decipher it.

The sheets of typescript should be numbered in one sequence in the top right-hand corner. If a sheet is added after 165, 165 should be changed to 165a, the new sheet numbered 165b, and 164 should carry note, '165a–b follow', so that it is immediately clear whether anything is missing. If a page is deleted, write on page 165 'no 166' or '167 follows'. If there are many insertions and deletions, renumber the whole typescript.

The typescript should contain everything that is to be printed, except for the index; that is, it should contain not only the main text but also the material to precede and follow it, including title page, contents list, any preface, dedication, acknowledgements, appendixes and bibliography, as well as all the illustrations, their captions and acknowledgements. Send with the typescript an inventory showing the number of sheets of typescript, listing any additional material to be provided, and giving particulars of any illustrations. If the material is in more than one package, each one should carry your name and address, and the book title.

Any correction at a later stage is expensive and may delay the book, so read your typescript critically before sending it to your publisher. If possible, ask a colleague to read it too; he may well notice some points you have overlooked, because he can read it with fresh eyes. In any case you should look at your punctuation and paragraphing; see that quotations and numbers (such as dates, quantities, page numbers) are accurate; compare the contents list with the chapter headings, and the illustrations with their captions and the relevant text; check all numbering to see that no pages, tables, equations, etc., are missing or wrongly numbered, that all notes to the text or tables have a number or symbol in the text or table and that no notes are missing.

Illustrations

Copy for illustrations may be provided either in a form suitable for direct photographic reproduction (camera copy) or in a rough form that will require redrawing before it can be reproduced. You should discuss with your publisher at an early stage how many and what kinds of illustrations your book needs. He can tell you whether the photographs you have are suitable for reproduction, and in what form you should present any diagrams.

Keep all the illustrations together, with the list of captions; do not insert them at the relevant point in your typescript. Label each one with your name, the title of the book and the illustration number, and mark the best position for each in the margin of the typescript.

Illustrations should be numbered in arabic. Your publisher will tell you whether photographs should be numbered in a separate sequence from maps and diagrams, and whether the numbering sequence should run throughout the book or start afresh in each chapter (Fig. 5.1 being the first diagram in Chapter 5).

In the text you should refer to all illustrations by number, as the physical limitations of a page may make it impossible to place each one near to the relevant sentence.

Diagrams and maps

Diagrams and maps should be kept simple, with the minimum of labelling, but make sure that all necessary labels are there, for example that the axes of graphs are labelled and the units defined.

Your diagrams must be clear and accurate: the draughtsman is a copier, not an interpreter.

For maps provide an accurate sketch map (with a scale and north point where appropriate) showing essential boundaries, contours, roads, etc. The draughtsman also needs a typed list of names consistent in spelling with the text and arranged in separate columns for countries, provinces, towns, rivers, etc., because a different size or kind of type may be used for each category. Photocopies of similar maps or source references to maps in other books will also be useful.

Check your maps and diagrams carefully before sending them to your publisher; make sure that they contain all, and only, the necessary information, and that the spelling, capitalisation and hyphenation are the same as in the text. Groups of diagrams that should be kept to the same scale should be labelled accordingly.

Camera copy

Illustrations for reproduction must be packed carefully, as any marks on them may reproduce. Large

4

diagrams may be rolled, *not* folded, but photographs are best packed flat between thick pieces of card.

Consult your publisher before drawing diagrams for reproduction. It is most important that the drawings are the right size and the lines the right thickness to allow for the required photographic reduction in size. Artwork is usually larger than the finished printed image, partly because it is easier to draw on a larger scale and partly because the photographic reduction helps to minimise any tiny imperfections in the drawings.

Many publishers prefer to receive unlettered artwork, so that the labels may be typeset to match the text; in that case show the lettering on a photocopy of the artwork. If your publisher has asked you to letter the artwork, follow his instructions about size and style of lettering.

Photographs

You should provide high-quality, sharp, black-and-white glossy prints with clear contrast in tonal values, detail visible in both highlights and shadows, and an uncluttered background. Matt or 'pebble-dash' prints, photocopies or illustrations from other publications will not reproduce well and should be avoided.

Photographic prints should be handled by the edges, as the surface area will be marked by fingerprints, which will then distort reproduction. They should be kept between pieces of stiff card a little larger than the prints, so that the corners do not become dog-eared. Do not secure them with paperclips, which may scratch the surface and will almost certainly dent it; such dents cast a minute shadow that cannot be eliminated photographically.

For the same reason, avoid writing on the back of the print. Your name, the book title and illustration number should be typed or written on a slip of paper which can be attached to the back of the photograph with a little rubber solution (e.g. Cow gum). Other instructions should be written on a photocopy of the photograph if possible, or otherwise on an overlay (a flap of tracing paper fastened by a strip of adhesive tape to the back of the photograph and covering the front of it) using a felt-tip pen. The corners of the print should be marked on the front of the overlay, to indicate the correct alignment in case the overlay should slip.

The top of the picture should be identified if there is any possibility of confusion. If a particular part of a photograph should not (or need not) be included in the printed illustration, the relevant area should be indicated on the photocopy or overlay, as should any letters, arrows, scale-bars, etc., to be superimposed on the photograph.

Captions

Type captions as a double-spaced list. Explanatory material should be transferred from diagrams to their captions, where practicable. Your publisher will tell you whether the acknowledgement of the source should be included in the captions or in a list of illustrations or sources.

Spelling and other conventions

Inconsistencies will irritate and possibly mislead the reader. Follow your publisher's style guide on these points; or, if you have no such guide, decide on your own system before the final draft is typed.

Spelling and accents

Some alternative spellings that are often inconsistent are:

    acknowledgement/acknowledgment
    biased/biassed
    connection/connexion
    co-operate/cooperate
    co-ordinate/coordinate
    dispatch/despatch
    elite/élite
    encyclopedia/encyclopaedia
    focused/focussed
    inquiry/enquiry
    -ise/-ize
    judgement/judgment
    medieval/mediaeval
    premiss/premise
    regime/régime
    role/rôle

You should of course follow the original spelling when quoting other people's work or giving the titles of other publications, but if non-standard spellings must be retained elsewhere they should be mentioned in a covering note.

Watch out for place-name spellings and use a consistent form, e.g. Basle or Basel.

If you want accents on any letters please mark them throughout the typescript. Indicate æ and œ ligatures thus: a͡e, o͡e. Especially with east European and the more exotic languages, it is unlikely that the publisher or typesetter will be able to check the accuracy of accents; it is therefore the author's particular responsibility to make sure that his system of accents is sound and consistent, and that any transliteration system is a generally accepted one and applied throughout; a note explaining the system may be necessary.

Hyphens

Hyphenate consistently or provide a list of preferred forms. Hyphens should be used only to avoid possible misunderstanding, e.g. re-cover and recover, deep blue sea and deep-blue sea.

En (or N) rules

En rules are slightly longer than hyphens; you will see them printed in pairs of numbers such as '1914–18'. They may be used to imply 'and' or 'to' in such phrases as 'French–English dictionary', 'London–Glasgow railway', 'farmer–poet', 'Brown–Robinson theory'. The publisher or typesetter may not know whether Brown-Robinson is one hyphenated name or two people; so if the sense requires an en rule please write N over the typed hyphen.

Capitals

Use capitals sparingly. Once you have decided on a system, apply it consistently, because it may be difficult for your publisher to apply a system which depends on the sense in which you use a particular word such as 'socialist' or 'conservative'.

Italic type

Italic should be used for foreign words in an English sentence, except in the following cases: the names of organisations such as political parties, ministries, commercial firms, and of streets and buildings; words now naturalised; common abbreviations (i.e., e.g., etc.); and quotations.

Other uses of italic are: for titles of periodicals and books (other than books of the Bible); for names of genera and species; for paintings; for operas, plays and films; and for names of ships. The use of italic for emphasis should be kept to a minimum.

When names that are normally italicised appear in capitalised or italic headings the publisher will probably enclose them in single quotation marks, e.g. SYMBOLISM IN 'THE MERCHANT OF VENICE', *A visit to H.M.S. 'Victory'*; foreign words are usually left undifferentiated in such cases.

Possessives and apostrophes

Be consistent in your inclusion or omission of an 's' after the apostrophe in possessives of names ending in 's' in the singular. It is usual to include the second 's' except when the last syllable is pronounced 'iz', e.g. Bridges', Moses' but James's, Thomas's. It is included after names which end in a silent 's', e.g. Rabelais's.

The apostrophe is best omitted in plurals such as 1960s and N.C.O.s.

Measurements

In general all measurements should be given in metric units: 4 m, 3 kg, 80 °C. If readers are unlikely to be very familiar with metric measurements, give the measurement in miles or tons, etc., followed by the metric equivalent in round brackets.

Numbers

Numbers expressing precise quantities or compared with others in statistical discussion should be in figures rather than words, as should numbers used for identification, such as page numbers. Other numbers up to 100 should be in words: five hospitals, twenty years ago, seventy-four years old; but 105 men, 314 women. Series of numbers should usually be in figures, e.g. '79 sheep and 108 cows', not 'seventy-nine sheep and 108 cows'. Use words rather than figures to start a sentence.

Use '0.15', not '.15'. Be consistent in your use of commas or spaces in thousands. The three systems are:

	4 digits	5 or more digits
	4999	14 999
	4999	14,999
	4,999	14,999

though, in columns of figures, 4- and 5-digit numbers will have to be treated consistently. Use the first of the three systems in scientific writing.

The second of a pair of numbers other than quantities should be abbreviated, except for the numbers 11 to 19, which retain the 1, e.g. 101–2, 130–1, but 111–12 and 1914–18.

If you have to refer to billions, say whether you are using the word in the British or the American sense.

Dates

Dates should appear in the form 18 September 1927, 1830s, nineteenth century (hyphenated when used as an adjective), 500 B.C. but A.D. 500.

Write 1967–8, not 1967–1968 or 1967–68; but 1914–15. In B.C. references the full dates must be given, e.g. 250–245 B.C.; 250–45 B.C. means something different. Use 'between 1971 and 1975' and 'from 1971 until 1975' or just '1971–5', but not 'between 1971–5' or 'from 1971–5'.

If you are not using the modern calendar or are adopting a special system (e.g. astronomical), make this clear either in a general note or at each occurrence.

Abbreviations and contractions

Avoid unnecessary abbreviations, and see that any unfamiliar ones are explained at their first occurrence or in a list.

No full stop is necessary where the contraction includes the first and last letter of the singular (Dr, Mme, St), or in abbreviated units, or in MS, MSS and per cent. The stop may also be omitted in sets of initials pronounced as a word (e.g. NATO, UNESCO) or in all sets of capital initials. The plural of m, kg and other abbreviated units is the same as the singular.

Be consistent in your use of 'per cent' and '%'; 'per cent' may be used in the text, but '%' is to be preferred in tables.

Cross-references

Cross-references to illustrations, tables, etc., should be completed and checked before you send your typescript to your publisher. Cross-references to the pages of your own book cannot, of course, be completed until page proofs are available, and should therefore be kept to a minimum. For essential cross-references type p. ooo or pp. ooo–oo, as a signal to insert the correct reference in the proof.

Be consistent in your use of capitals or lower-case for such words as chapter, appendix, table, fig., vol.

Headings

Do not use more than three kinds of heading within a chapter; the more kinds there are, the more difficult it will be for the reader to distinguish one grade from another. Headings should be typed with a capital for the first word and proper names only; distinguish the grades of heading by pencilling 'A' in the margin beside the major headings, 'B' and 'C' beside the second and third grades.

Headlines or running heads

It is usual to have the title of the chapter on the left-hand page and of a major chapter subdivision on the right-hand, or the part title on the left and the chapter title on the right. If the titles are likely to be too long to fit across the top of the page, provide a list of short forms.

Tables

Tables may be typed on separate sheets or in the text; any notes should be typed immediately below each one. Tables of more than four lines should be numbered – and referred to in the text by number rather than 'as follows' – because the printer may not be able to place them in the ideal position. Mark the desirable position in the margin if the tables are typed on separate sheets.

Vertical and horizontal lines are kept to a minimum in printed tables. If any are essential in your own tables tell your publisher when you send the typescript.

To avoid correction at proof stage do check your tables carefully. Are they in the form that the reader will find most helpful? Will he be able to compare one set of values with another? Are all units, percentages and totals identified? Do the totals tally with the individual values? Are the sources given in the same form for each table?

Quotations

All quotations should be typed double-spaced. Use single quotation marks except for quotations within 'single-quoted' passages, which have double.

Prose quotations occupying more than five lines of typescript – if there are many of them – will probably be distinguished typographically from the rest of the text. The typist should start each such quotation on a fresh line and indent the whole quotation, say five spaces from the margin; the first line of any new paragraphs after the beginning of the quotation should be indented a further five spaces; the first line following the quotation should not be indented unless it begins a new paragraph. Such quotations may be printed without quotation marks, in which case quotations within them will take single quotation marks.

Verse quotations of more than one line should be centred, and should show the poet's indention scheme, if any, clearly; they do not need quotation marks. If there is likely to be any doubt, for example with foreign languages, quotations should be labelled 'verse' or 'prose' in the margin.

The publisher and typesetter will follow the typescript exactly for spelling, capitalisation, punctuation and the use of italic in quotations; but certain points of house style are usually standardised. For example, punctuation is likely to be placed after the closing quotation mark except for a dash, exclamation mark or question mark belonging to the quoted words, or a full stop if the quotation is or ends with a grammatically complete sentence starting with a capital letter. Ellipses (three dots to indicate an omission) may be omitted at the beginning and end of a quotation, and so may a full stop before or after an ellipsis in the middle of a quotation; if you wish these to be retained say so, and make clear whether the full stop precedes or follows the ellipsis. Use square brackets for any explanatory insertions or substitutions within quotations.

Check all quotations very carefully before sending your typescript to your publisher. If you are quoting a large amount from modern editions (e.g. in an anthology), use clear photocopies of the relevant printed pages, pasted onto standard typescript sheets, to avoid introducing typing errors. If you are quoting poetry, indicate whether a break at the foot of a page is an accident of layout or a deliberate stanza break.

Copyright permissions

The following is intended only as a general introduction to procedures for gaining permissions for the use within your text of material (whether text or photographs or diagrams, etc.) which is in copyright but of which you are not the copyright holder.

To begin with, there are three things to establish. First, whether it is you or the publisher who is to write for permissions: this you will find from your contract or by conversation with your publisher. Secondly, whether or not a particular quotation is out of copyright. (In the U.K., a work is in copyright until fifty years after the author's death, or, if not published during his lifetime, for fifty years after first publication. Other countries have other periods of copyright: your publisher will give you further details.) Thirdly, whether or not permission is necessary. In the main, it *is* necessary to write for permission to the copyright owner or his agent, but there are certain uses for which permission is not needed, particularly, in this context, 'fair dealing' for purposes of criticism and review, and the use of a 'non-substantial' part. It is impossible to give any rules on these uses (for further information on this, see Christopher Scarles, *Copyright*, in this series). It is often the case that a short quotation need not be the subject of permission (being 'non-substantial') and it can happen that a quite lengthy passage, in the context of a work of criticism or review, is also not subject to permission. But each case is different, and you should talk to your publisher in order to establish his normal working rules on substantial part, fair dealing, and any other relevant questions.

You should keep a record of your sources – either for your own use or, if your publisher is clearing permissions, for you to send to him with your final typescript.

The letter requesting permission should be written to the original publisher of the material and should identify the passage by providing an exact reference for it, either by quoting the opening and closing phrases or by supplying a copy of the whole passage. You should be quite explicit about the rights required. Inevitably, they will be non-exclusive, but should they be for one edition or so many copies?, for the first and any future editions?, for a limited territory?, in English only?, in other languages? – and so on. Only your publisher can give this information in an exact form, and what he says would normally reflect the rights you are granting him in your contract with him.

If you are clearing permissions, your publisher may require you to send him all relevant correspondence for checking and retention for further reference. Whoever clears permissions, the author is usually expected to pay for them. The normal exceptions to this are books which rely heavily on copyright material (anthologies, for example), where there is often a considerable sum involved. In these cases the publisher may pay, but this would tend to affect the terms of his contract with the author.

Footnotes and endnotes

Discuss the notes with your publisher at an early stage. The cost of notes can be out of proportion to the use made of them by the reader, and may remove scholarly books from the reach of those who want them. Before adding a note, ask yourself whether the information could be worked into the text or omitted.

Notes can be almost entirely avoided if the author–date system of bibliographical references (see p. 18) is employed: it is suited to most books in which all the references are to books and journals, and it is used not only by scientists but by an increasing number of writers in the humanities. If the author–date system is not suitable, it may still be possible to keep down the number of notes by putting short references (such as a series of page references to the same work) in the text. To keep the notes as short as possible, full publication details – series, total number of volumes, publisher, place and date of publication – may be omitted provided there is a full bibliography.

In a work for a scholarly audience some acquaintance with the background and the literature can be assumed; and often the only statements that need support are those likely to be contested.

Notes may be placed at the foot of the page or at the end of the book (preceding the bibliography and index); they are more difficult to find at the end of the relevant chapters, and are usually placed there only in journals, symposia, etc., where each chapter is an independent work and may be made available as an offprint.

Books with footnotes are more complicated to produce, because some adjustment is necessary at page make-up stage to ensure that all the notes fall on the same page as their text references. Only information that is immediately necessary to the reader's understanding, but which cannot be incorporated in the text, merits a footnote; if most of the notes are references which readers do not need to consult immediately, they are all best placed at the end of the book, leaving the text pages uncluttered.

Note numbers in the text should not be enclosed in brackets unless a book contains mathematics. They should come at a break in the sense and follow the punctuation. See p. 1 about the typing of the notes themselves.

Bibliographical references

The short-title system
References in the text and notes
(i) *Books*

Give the full details when the book is first mentioned, as follows:

(1) author's initials or forename (in the same form as in the bibliography), followed by
(2) author's surname
(3) title of book, underlined for italic except for unpublished theses (the titles of which should be

placed between single quotation marks) and manuscript sources; be consistent about capitalisation

(4) editor, compiler or translator, if any. If there is no author, the editor or compiler will appear in (1) and (2)

(5) series, if any, plus volume number in the series. The series name should not usually be underlined

(6) edition (if not the first)

(7) number of volumes, publication place, publisher and date (all in round brackets). Publication places should usually be anglicised

(8) volume (if more than one) and page number. If only the relevant volume was published in that year, the volume number should precede the place. It is usual to include 'vol.' and 'p.' (or 'pp.' if more than one page), and to shorten the second number (except those between 11 and 19) in a pair of numbers, e.g. pp. 508–9, 512–16. It is better to give the first and last page number rather than 'pp. 512ff' or 'pp. 512 *et seq.*'

The references should be punctuated as in the following examples:

J. A. Hazel, *The growth of the cotton trade in Lancashire*, 2nd edn (4 vols., London, Textile Press, 1956–7), vol. 3, p. 2

P. Carter, *Frognal to Englands Lane*, London Street Names Series, vol. 45 (London, Textile Press, 1938), p. 45

Items (4)–(7) may be omitted if the book is included in the bibliography, though dates of publication may be given if relevant to the argument. If the author's name and the book title are given in the text, his initials and the publication date (if either of these is needed) could be given in the text as well, thus saving a note.

Later references should contain the author's surname and a short title; or the author's name may be sufficient if there is only one entry under that surname in the bibliography. *Op. cit.* and *loc. cit.* should not be used: if there is only one book by a particular author, *op. cit.* is unnecessary; if there is more than one, the use of *op. cit.* may involve the reader in looking back through many notes to find a more explicit reference. So the second reference should contain:

(1) author's surname
(2) short title (if necessary)
(3) volume and page number

e.g. Hazel, *Cotton trade*, vol. 4, p. 102

(ii) *Articles in books*

The first reference is as for a book, but item (3) on p. 14 above is amplified as follows:

(a) title of article, not underlined but usually in single quotation marks and with a capital only for the first word and any proper nouns (italic words within the title remain italic; words in quotation marks take double quotation marks)
(b) 'in'
(c) editor's name followed by '(ed.)', or '(eds.)' if there is more than one editor
(d) title of book underlined for italic

Noam Chomsky, 'Explanatory models in linguistics' in J. A. Fodor and J. J. Katz (eds.), *The structure of language* (Englewood Cliffs, N.J., Prentice-Hall, 1964), pp. 50–118

or (c) may follow (d), in which case the editor's name will be preceded by 'ed.' (edited by) and 'in' may be omitted, e.g.

Noam Chomsky, 'Explanatory models in linguistics', *The structure of language*, ed. J. A. Fodor and J. J. Katz (Englewood Cliffs, N.J., Prentice-Hall, 1964), pp. 50–118

If the book is listed under its editor in the bibliography, the subsequent reference will be:

Chomsky, 'Explanatory models' in Fodor and Katz, *Structure of language*, p. 72.

or the short title of the article and/or the book may be omitted if there will be no confusion with another publication:

Chomsky in Fodor and Katz, p. 72

If the book is listed in the bibliography under the author of the article, subsequent references will probably be:

(iii) *Journal articles*

The first reference should contain:

(1) author's initials or forename, followed by
(2) author's surname
(3) title of article, not underlined but usually in single quotation marks and with a capital only for the first word and any proper names (italic words within the title remain italic; words in quotation marks take double quotation marks)
(4) title of journal, underlined; be consistent about capitalisation
(5) place, if there is more than one journal with the same name
(6) volume number in roman or arabic figures ('vol.' not needed), plus issue number if the volume is not paginated continuously
(7) year, in round brackets
(8) relevant page number(s) ('p.', 'pp.' not needed)

punctuated as follows:

J. L. Carr, 'Uncertainty and monetary theory', *Economics*, 2 (1956), 82–9

Later references should contain the author's surname and either the journal title, volume number, etc., or else a shortened form of the article title:

Carr, 'Uncertainty and monetary theory', p. 82
or
Carr, *Economics*, 2 (1956), 82

If you use journal abbreviations which may not be familiar to your readers, provide a list.

(iv) *Biblical references*

Use the form Genesis 16.5 for biblical references.

(v) *Manuscripts*

Use 'fol.', 'fols.' (not f., ff.) for 'folios'; 'r' and 'v' for 'recto' and 'verso' should not be raised or underlined.

Bibliography

A bibliography may serve as a guide to sources or to further reading; but if readers are to be able to follow up references in the text or notes, it should not be too much subdivided: the reader will not want to look through three or more alphabetical lists to find a particular author. Division into manuscript sources, official publications, other primary sources, and secondary sources, should be the maximum necessary.

The bibliography should be arranged alphabetically and the author's surname should therefore precede his initials. Keep the order within each entry, and also the capitalisation and punctuation, consistent throughout the bibliography. The entries are punctuated differently from the references in footnotes; the examples given above would appear in the bibliography as follows:

Carr, J. L. 'Uncertainty and monetary theory', *Economics*, 2 (1956), 82–9.

Carter, P. *Frognal to Englands Lane*, London Street Names Series, vol. 45, London, Textile Press, 1938.

Chomsky, Noam, 'Explanatory models in linguistics' in J. A. Fodor and J. J. Katz (eds.), *The structure of language*, Englewood Cliffs, N.J., Prentice-Hall, 1964, pp. 50–118.

Hazel, J. A. *The growth of the cotton trade in Lancashire*, 2nd edn, 4 vols., London, Textile Press, 1956–7.

Note that references to articles, whether in journals or books, should include the first and last page numbers of the article.

Check your notes against the bibliography, because it will confuse and irritate the reader if the details given are not the same.

The author–date system
References in the text

The author's name, date of publication and page reference (if one is needed) are given in round brackets, e.g. 'the synthesis of amino acids (D'Arcy, 1920, pp. 131–8) amazed...'. The reference may be simplified still further, by omitting the first comma and substituting a colon for the second and 'pp.', e.g. 'D'Arcy 1920: 131–8'. If the author's name forms part of the sentence, it is not repeated in the reference, e.g. 'the synthesis of amino acids by D'Arcy (1920, pp. 131–8) amazed...'. If the author published two or more works in one year, these are labelled '1920a' etc.

The names of two joint authors are always given. Three and four joint authors are always given in full the first time and thereafter *et al.* may be used. Five or more names can be given as *et al.* from the start.

Where several references are cited together in the text they may be placed in alphabetical or chronological order, or in order of importance, but the same system should be used throughout.

Be consistent in your inclusion or omission of a comma between the author's name and the date, your use of '&' or 'and' for joint authors, and your use of '*et al.*'

The references should be in strict alphabetical order by author, irrespective of the number of authors per paper (e.g. Eckstein, Brown & Jones comes before Eckstein & Jones). Papers by the same author(s) should be in chronological order. Repeat all the authors' names unless the authorship is exactly the same as for the preceding paper. Be consistent in your use of '&' or 'and' for joint authors.

The date (followed by 'a', etc., if necessary) immediately follows the name of the author(s), so that the reader can easily find 'D'Arcy 1920a'.

Article titles, if given, have a capital only for the first word and are not in quotation marks. Journal titles should be given in full; and both book and journal titles should be underlined. The first and last page numbers of every article should be given.

Eckstein, P. & Zuckerman, S. 1960. Morphology of the reproductive tract. In *Marshall's physiology of reproduction*, ed. A. S. Parkes, vol. 1, pp. 43–154. London, Longman.

Morgan, R. 1967. The personal orientation of long-stay psychiatric patients. *British Journal of Psychiatry*, 113: 847–59.

Before sending your typescript to your publisher, check all the text references against the list, to make sure that the list is complete and that names and dates are given correctly in the text.

Science and mathematics

Use SI units, as recommended in *Quantities, units and symbols* published by the Royal Society of London, e.g. m, kg, s, mol, μm (*not* μ), nm (*not* Å), lx (*not* ft-candles), min, K (*not* °K). Remember that units have neither plurals nor full stops. Compound units should be typed as, for example, mg dm^{-3} *or* mg/dm^3, but not both.

Handwritten copy should be kept to an absolute minimum and must be unambiguous. Check especially that it is clear whether letters such as v, s, c and x are capital or lower-case, and that 1 /I/l, oh/zero, x/multiplication sign, v/Greek nu are clearly distinguished.

Underline letters used as mathematical symbols, but not expressions such as 'cos', 'log' and 'lim', the differential operator 'd' (as in dy/dx), the exponential 'e' and other pure numbers, and subscripts that are not themselves physical or mathematical quantities. Use a wavy underline for bold characters. Make sure that subscripts and superscripts are immediately recognisable as such. Identify at first occurrence (in pencil in the margin) all special characters such as script or foreign letters and mathematical symbols.

Consult your publisher if you need to use unusual characters; complicated notation can cause problems for the typesetter. It may also confuse the reader, so define each symbol when you first introduce it, and explain any subscript labels. When you have completed the book, check that you have used the notation consistently.

Chemistry

Names of chemical compounds should follow the approved (IUPAC/IUB) system. Use ^{14}C for heavy carbon, ^{3}H for tritium; for labelled compounds use [^{14}C] thymine, etc. Use SO_4^{2-}, Fe^{3+}, etc., *not* $SO_4^=$ Fe^{+++}.

Reproduction of chemical structures in running text can cause difficulty, so use the most compact form of notation, such as $(CH_3)_2CO$, unless it is absolutely necessary to give a chemical structure explicitly.

Biology

Check that your use of Latin names for species accurate and up to date. Authorities are rarely necessary, but if used should be given after the introduction of each name.

Correcting proofs

When the book has been typeset you will receive a proof and your typescript, so that you can check that the typesetter has followed your typescript accurately and that the illustrations and tables have been sensibly positioned. This stage should not be regarded as an opportunity to rewrite parts of the book: alterations are expensive and may necessitate another proof stage to check that they have been carried out properly. Virtually every change, however small, entails resetting a complete line. If you must change one or two letters, substitute a word or words of the same number of characters (letters and spaces) in the same line or an adjacent one; otherwise the typesetter will have to move words from line to line until he can make up the space lost or gained.

Do not read proofs only for sense; look at every letter and punctuation mark. You may find it easier to notice errors if you place a strip of paper across the page, and move it down a line at a time, to isolate the line you are reading from those that follow. If there is a glaring error, your eye may leap over the intervening words; so read the whole line again when you have marked the correction. Sometimes a typesetter's error can change one word to another; this is more difficult to notice, e.g. 'causal relationship' can become 'casual relationship', 'ingenuous' 'ingenious', 'unexceptionable' 'unexceptional', 'alternatively' 'alternately'.

See that no opening or closing quotation marks or brackets are missing. Check the preliminary pages, headings, headlines, and the numerical sequence of pages, notes (and their text indicators), sections, tables, illustrations, equations, etc. See that illustrations and tables are sensibly placed. Add the missing page numbers to the contents list and any lists of illustrations or tables, checking the titles against the captions or table headings at the same time. Cross-references to pages must be filled in, and all references to illustrations, tables, section and equation numbers cross-checked.

Mark wrong founts (letters in the wrong type or size), wrong indention, unequal spacing between words or lines, and other printing faults. End-of-line word breaks should be left unaltered unless they are actually misleading or startlingly wrong.

If some corrections to the text will affect page references in the index – for example if a table is wrongly placed and has to be moved from page to page – work out what the page numbers should be and send your publisher a note of the entries that must be checked. If you are not indexing your book yourself, note for the indexer any corrections to the spelling of proper names, so that he can incorporate them in the index typescript.

See that each illustration tallies with its caption. If an illustration has been reduced for reproduction check that any scale given in the form of a magnification or reduction in the caption has been altered. See that the foot or any turned illustration is at the right-hand side of the page.

How to mark corrections

The typesetter runs his eye down the margin to see which lines contain alterations; so each correction needs not only a mark in the text but also the correct symbol written in the margin, level with the error; if the line contains more than one mistake, write the corrections in the same order as in the text, separated by oblique strokes. Use British Standard symbols (see pp. 23–5), write your corrections clearly, taking special care over proper names, foreign words, technical terms and symbols.

Always make it absolutely clear how much is to be deleted: a carelessly written diagonal stroke through one letter can pass through part of its two neighbours and the typesetter may not be able to tell whether you are deleting one letter or three. If you delete a hyphen, make it clear whether you want one word or two instead; if you add one or more letters between two foreign words, show whether the letters form a separate word or are to be added to the preceding or following word.

Answer any typesetter's queries *briefly*: merely cross out the question mark if you agree with his suggestion; cross out the whole suggestion if you disagree.

The typesetter will charge for all corrections which are not his own errors and colour-coded as such. Th

Instruction	Textual mark	Marginal mark
Leave unchanged	--- under characters to remain	Ⓥ
Remove extraneous marks	encircle marks to be removed	✗
Delete	/ through character or ⊢──⊣ through word(s)	♂
Delete and close up	⌒I through character or ⊟ through word(s)	⌒♂
Insert in text the matter indicated in the margin	⋏	new matter followed by ⋏
Substitute character or word(s)	/ through character or ⊢──⊣ through word(s)	new character or new word(s)
Substitute or insert character in 'superior' position	/ through character or ⋏ where required	Ɣ under character e.g. ²Ɣ
Substitute or insert character in 'inferior' position	/ through character or ⋏ where required	⋏ over character e.g. ⋏₂
Substitute or insert full stop or decimal point, comma, semi-colon, etc.	/ through character or ⋏ where required	⊙/ ,/ ;/ ⊙/)/
Substitute or insert single or double quotation marks, or apostrophe	/ through character or ⋏ where required	⁶/ and/or ⁹/ ⁶⁶/ and/or ⁹⁹/
Substitute or insert hyphen rule oblique	/ through character or ⋏ where required	⊢─⊣ 1en (give length required) Ⓞ
Wrong fount. Replace by character(s) of correct fount	encircle character(s) to be changed	⊗
Change damaged character(s)	encircle character(s) to be changed	✗

Instruction	Textual mark	Marginal mark
Set in or change to italic	____ under character(s) to be set or changed	⌐⌐/
Set in or change to capital letter(s)	≡≡≡ under character(s) to be set or changed	≡
Set in or change to small capital letter(s)	== under character(s) to be set or changed	=
Set in or change to bold type	∿∿ under character(s) to be set or changed	∿
Set in or change to bold italic type	____∿∿ under character(s) to be set or changed	⌐⌐/∿∿
Change capital letters to lower-case letters	encircle character(s) to be changed	≠
Change small capital letters to lower-case letters	encircle character(s) to be changed	≠
Change italic to upright type	encircle character(s) to be changed	⌐/
Invert type	encircle character to be inverted	↺
Start new paragraph	⌐	⌐
Run on (no new paragraph)	⌒	⌒
Transpose characters or words	⌐⌐ between characters or words, numbered when necessary	⌐⌐
Transpose a number of lines	____ 3 ____ 2 ____ 1	rules extend from margin into text with each line to be transplanted numbered in correct sequence
Centre	[enclosing matter to be centred]	[ ]

Instruction	Textual mark	Marginal mark
Indent	⌐⌐	⌐⌐
Cancel indent	⊩⌐	⌐⌐
Take over character(s), word(s) or line to next line, column or page	⌐⌐	textual mark surrounds matter to be taken over and extends into margin
Take back character(s), word(s), or line to previous line, column or page	⌐	textual mark surrounds matter to be taken back and extends into margin
Correct vertical alignment	‖	‖
Correct horizontal alignment	single line above and below mis-aligned matter	=
Close up. Delete space between characters or words	linking ⌣ characters	⌣
Insert space between characters	| between characters	Y
Insert space between words	Y between words	Y
Reduce space between characters	| between characters	⋀
Reduce space between words	⋀ between words	⋀
Make space appear equal between characters or words	| between characters or words	Y
Close up to normal interline spacing	{ each side of column linking lines }	

2094009

Extracts from BS 5621 Part 2 1976 are reproduced by permission of the British Standards Institution, 2 Park Street, London W1A 2BS, from whom complete copies can be obtained.

following is the standard system of colour-coding, which is used ~~for~~ to assess liability for correction changes:

> green: typesetters' own marks (corrections and queries)
>
> red: author's or publisher's correction of typesetter's errors
>
> Blue or black: author's and publisher's own alterations (including any carried out in response to the typesetter's queries)

Some publishers ask authors to use blue for their own alterations and black for any publisher's errors (errors of omission or commission made during editing or copy-editing), insertion cross-references and headlines

Making an index

The following is only a brief guide. For further information read M. D. Anderson's Book indexing in this series.

Your publisher will tell you how many printed pages the index should occupy, and what this means in terms of entries. The index should contain topics as well as proper names. any entry containing more though you should not go to the other extreme and make a sub-entry for every page number. A single than about six page references should be subdivided, reference covering a span of more than about ten pages (e.g. 110/25) should probably be subdivided.

Although you cannot complete the index until you have the page proofs, it can save time later if you compile the entries and sub-entries from the typescript, revising the entries and changing the page numbers when you receive the page proofs.

It is better to start by over-indexing than by under-indexing: is it far quicker to delete an unwanted entry or to combine two or more sub-entries than to chase back through the text for an entry which turns out to be necessary.

But do not index passing mentions which give no information about the topic or person. Do not index the foreword or preface unless it gives information pertinent to the subject of the book.

Corrected page; see opposite.

following is the standard system of colour-codi
which is used to assess liability for correction
charges:

> green: typesetter's own marks (corrections and
> queries)
>
> red: author's or publisher's correction of type-
> setter's errors
>
> blue or black: author's and publisher's own alter-
> ations (including any carried out in response to
> the typesetter's queries)

Some publishers ask authors to use blue for their own
alterations and black for any publisher's errors
(errors of omission or commission made during
editing or copy-editing), insertion of cross-references
and headlines.

Making an index

The following is only a brief guide. For further information read M. D. Anderson's *Book indexing* in this
series.

Your publisher will tell you how many printed
pages the index should occupy, and what this means
in terms of entries. The index should contain topics
as well as proper names. Any entry containing more
than about six page references should be subdivided,
though you should not go to the other extreme and
make a sub-entry for every page number. A single
reference covering a span of more than about ten
pages (e.g. 110–25) should probably be subdivided.

Although you cannot complete the index until you
have the page proofs, it can save time later if you
compile the entries and sub-entries from the typescript, revising the entries and changing the page
numbers when you receive the page proofs.

It is better to start by over-indexing than by under-
indexing: it is far quicker to delete an unwanted
entry or to combine two or more sub-entries than to
chase back through the text for an entry which turns
out to be necessary. But do not index passing mentions which give no information about the topic or
person.

Do not index the foreword or preface unless it gives
information pertinent to the subject of the book.

Footnotes should be indexed only if they give additional information about a topic or person not mentioned elsewhere on that page. Endnotes should be indexed only if they contain substantive information. Bibliographies and general lists of references are not indexed, though a list of references can double as an author index (see below).

What to use as the entry heading

The heading should be a noun (qualified or not) rather than an adjective or verb. Use a concrete, specific term in preference to a vague, general one. How specific an entry should be depends on the subject of the book: in a book on infectious diseases an entry 'disease' or 'infectious diseases' would be too long, and there should instead be entries for specific diseases, but in a book on demography it might well be more useful to have all the diseases grouped together.

Where there are two or more possible synonyms, use the one the reader is most likely to look up, and put *all* the relevant page numbers in that entry; do not put half of them under one synonym and half under another. If the two words are closely related but not synonyms, put the relevant references under each, with a cross-reference to the other.

When a word has more than one meaning, there should be a separate entry for each meaning, with an explanatory phrase to show which meaning is intended. Proper names should be separate entries rather than sub-entries:

London, 81–4, 91	*not* London, 81–4, 91
London, Jack, 184	Jack, 184
London School of Economics, 83	School of Economics, 83

Proper names

Saints, kings and popes are indexed under their forename, but places, institutions, acts of Parliament, book titles, etc., are placed under the first word after the article:

William IV, king of England *but* King William Street

Thérèse of Lisieux, St *but* St Louis, Missouri

Lewis, John *but* John Lewis Partnership Ltd

However, physical features are indexed under the second part of the name:

> Victoria, Lake *not* Lake Victoria

No entry should start with 'a' or 'the' except in an index of first lines. Exceptions to these rules are names in another language (Eilean Donan, Las Vegas), which are indexed under the first word.

Compound personal names, whether hyphenated or not, should be indexed under the first element of the surname:

> Vaughan Williams, Ralph *but* Maugham, W. Somerset

In French, Italian and German names, a preposition (de, da, von) follows the name but an article or compound of preposition and article (La, Du, Des) precedes the name. Names naturalised in Britain or the United States are usually indexed under the prefix:

> Goethe, J. S. von *but* De Quincey, Thomas

The form of the entry

The entry should not start with a capital letter unless it is a proper name or a term capitalised in the text. Keep the wording and punctuation to a minimum, provided the meaning is clear.

General page references should be grouped together immediately after the entry heading. Use 161–6 not 161ff or 161–66, and avoid *passim* unless there are a large number of general references to a person or topic in one section of a book. Distinguish between 65–6 (a continuous discussion of the topic) and 65, 66 (two separate mentions).

References to footnotes should be in the form 55n or, if the footnotes are long or numerous, 55n2. References to endnotes should include the page on which the note appears, and also the note number, because there will be several notes on each page.

There should be no punctuation at the end of an entry.

Sub-entries

Sub-entries may be arranged in alphabetical or chronological order, whichever is more suitable for the subject matter. The alphabetical order may disregard such words as 'and', 'at', 'in', 'of', so that the sub-entry need not be inverted in order to alphabetise the significant word. There should be no punctuation at the end of a sub-entry that occupies a separate line, or at the end of a block of sub-entries.

If there are no general page references, the entry heading should be separated from the first sub-entry by a colon if the sub-entries run on. Where the sub-entries are on separate lines, the first one should not run on from the entry heading:

page numbers	page numbers: in contents
in contents list, 18–19	list, 18–19; omission of,
omission of, 71, 192	71, 192

Sub-sub-entries usually run on after the relevant sub-entries; only in reference works are they set out on separate lines:

page numbers	page numbers: omission
omission of, 71, 192;	of, 71, 192, in prelimi-
in preliminary	nary pages, 101–2; pos-
pages 101–2	ition of, 16–17
position of, 16–17	

Cross-references If an entry is purely a cross-reference, it is usually in the form:

Britain, *see* United Kingdom

The words should be in the same order as in the entry to which it refers:

Bell, Currer, *see* Brontë, Charlotte
not   Bell, Currer, *see* Charlotte Brontë

If the cross-reference is part of an entry, it should be in the form '*see also*'. It may immediately follow the heading (in brackets) if it is important, or the last sub-entry if it is not. Cross-references from a sub-entry form part of that sub-entry.

Alphabetical order The order may be either word by word or letter by letter, counting only as far as the first comma and then starting again; but be careful to use the same system throughout.

Word-by-word	*Letter-by-letter*
Port, William	Port, William
Port Sunlight	Portinscale
Portinscale	Port Sunlight

M', Mc and Mac are all counted as Mac, St as Saint; but all other abbreviations are alphabetised as they are spelt. In abbreviations consisting of a set of initials separated by full stops, each letter counts as a separate word. Treat ä, å as a, ö as o.

'Sir' and other titles are ignored in alphabetising:

Jones, Sir John
Jones, Lionel

Author index If there is a list of references at the end of each chapter, the author index will usually distinguish those page numbers from text references, so that the reader can see at a glance where he can find the details of the publications cited.

If the author index is combined with the list of references, the page numbers in your own book may be set within square brackets or in italic to distinguish them from the page numbers in the reference itself.

Checking the index Before it is typed, check that the index is approximately the right length; then look at each entry and sub-entry and ask yourself:

(1) Is it necessary? Will it tell the reader anything? Will the reader of this kind of book look it up?
(2) Has the appropriate word or phrase been used for the entry? Is it clearly and concisely worded?
(3) Should the entry be combined with another entry?
(4) Does it overlap with a near-synonym? If so, the two entries should be more clearly defined, the page references checked to make sure which entry they belong to, and a cross-reference added to each entry.
(5) Are any further cross-references needed?
(6) Does each cross-reference refer to an entry which still exists? Is it correctly worded?
(7) Are there some entries which contain only sur-

names? If so add forenames or initials if possible.

(8) Is a note needed at the beginning of the index to explain any special points about the index?

Typing the index

The typescript should be *double-spaced* and single-column, with a margin of $1\frac{1}{2}$ inches (40 mm) at the left, and of 1 inch (25 mm) at the top, the right and the foot. If sub-entries are to occupy separate lines they should be indented two or three spaces from the entry heading, and all continuation lines (whether of entry or sub-entry) should be indented a further two or three. If sub-entries run straight on from the entry, all continuation lines should be indented two or three spaces. (See the examples on p. 30 above.) It is helpful to the typesetter if you can leave extra space before the start of entries for a new letter.

Check spellings, accents, page numbers and alphabetical order before you send the typescript to your publisher.